# WIZARD TRICKS

## TOPTHAT!Kids™

Copyright © 2002 Top That! Publishing plc
Tide Mill Way, Woodbridge, Suffolk, IP12 1AP, UK
www.topthatpublishing.com
Top That! Kids is a trademark of Top That! Publishing plc
All rights reserved

# Contents

**WIZARD'S ART**
- 4  Welcome to Wizard's School
- 6  Wizardly Wisdom
- 8  The Wizard's Box
- 10  Rituals and Codes
- 12  Wizard's Magic Table
- 14  Table Trickery

**TIME FOR TRICKS**
- 16  Cauldron Code
- 18  Vanishing Pouch
- 20  Crystal Ball
- 22  Magic Mirror
- 24  Morphology
- 25  Metamorphosis
- 26  Octagon Oracle
- 28  Wizard Stars
- 32  Coin Elevation
- 33  Evanescence
- 34  Potion Prediction
- 36  Wizard's Squeeze
- 38  Ropology
- 40  Wizard's Brew
- 42  Enchanted Key
- 43  Mind Meeting
- 44  Ancient Runes
- 46  Magic Magnetism
- 48  Rings of Moebius
- 50  Midas Touch
- 52  Wizard's Range
- 54  Magic Maths
- 56  Vanishing Point
- 58  Potion Trickery

**TEMPLATES AND TOKENS**
- 60  Cauldron Code
- 61  Octagon Oracle
- 62  Morphology
- 63  Potion Prediction
- 64  Ancient Runes

# Wizard's Art

# Welcome to the Wizard's School of Magic

In the days when dragons wandered the earth, a humble wizard's apprentice recorded the events which took place when the world's most powerful wizards gathered once again to share their knowledge with the Wizard's Council. The knowledge of these great wizards was recorded in one mystical book, named the Wizard's School of Magic.

The magic of the ages has brought this book to you. Look after it well and devote much time and effort to mastering the magic it contains. It is your responsibility to continue the traditions of the Wizard's Council.

Learn to discover and share the ancient magic that is within you, as you begin your journey through the tricks of the ages.

# Wizardly Wisdom

Essential tips collected from famous
wizards across the Earth and the centuries.

 Always prepare your props well in advance of a performance. Smudged paint and wet glue will detract from your wondrous wizardry.

 Organise a stage area in which to perform. Practise in this area, as it will make you feel more confident when you have an audience.

Make sure that mobile phones, pagers and land lines are switched off during your performance; they can be very distracting for you and your audience. It helps to set the scene if you have wizardly props around you.

The importance of practice should never be underestimated. The level of knowledge and skill a good wizard has is honed and perfected over centuries. When you perform a trick, therefore, it must not look as though you have only just learned it!

Every trick is so much more effective if it is performed smoothly and without any visible effort. A little time and patience will make you an even better wizard!

# The Wizard's Box

Use the items in your wizard's box wisely. They were collected from far and wide by the Wizard's Council, and are all you need to put on a fantastic show.

The Wizard's hat and wand have been handed down for many centuries from an apprentice about to graduate as a fully-fledged wizard, to his successor, an apprentice-in-training.
It is therefore very important that they are looked after. They must only be used when practising the art of wizardly magic and should not be worn or carried at any other time.

The Vanishing Pouch included in this kit was brought to the Wizard's Council by Meldrick the Mystical. It is used to make almost anything disappear.
It was cut from the cloth of Meldrick's magic cloak.

The pot of gold stars was presented to the Wizard's Council by the wizard Arman, who managed to capture the rare magical stars from the Cloud City of Orbis.

# Rituals and Codes

As an apprentice wizard, you are required to abide by the wizard's rituals and codes. The Council came up with a list of these, which were passed at the first gathering in the Cloud City of Orbis Summit. They are as follows:

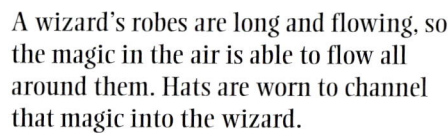

- A wizard's robes are long and flowing, so the magic in the air is able to flow all around them. Hats are worn to channel that magic into the wizard.

- To appear really professional, prepare your table and tricks well before the performance.

- Create your own magic words. The magic of the ages may have brought this volume to you, but it is your own magic that will make these tricks work.

- Never reveal how your magic works, unless to a fellow wizard.

Don't forget to give yourself a cool wizard name – use your imagination to think one up!

 Name the tricks you perform. If you have trouble remembering the order in which to perform your tricks, write the names of them down on a piece of paper before you perform and keep it close to you during your show.

 Practise each trick many times before you show it to anyone.

 Do not perform your tricks more than once in front of the same audience.

 Talk to the audience in between tricks and as you are setting up.

 Always end your performance with a smile and a bow. Be sure to thank your audience for coming.

# Wizard's Magic Table

For centuries wizards have used powerful tables to help them perform magic. Shrouded in mystery until now, you can make your own wizard's magic table by following these simple steps!

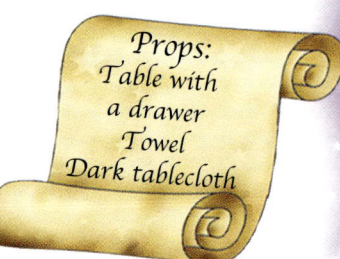

Props:
Table with a drawer
Towel
Dark tablecloth

**1** Take out the drawer from the table and pad the bottom with a fluffy towel. Cover the table with a dark tablecloth to make it look more mysterious.

2. Arrange the table so that the drawer is pointing away from your audience and you have a secret place in which to drop things or retrieve them.

3. When you stand behind your magical table, you should now be able to make use of this secret compartment, unseen by the audience!

*Wizard's Tip*
*Magic tables are an excellent place to keep props until you need them.*

# Table Trickery

If you don't have a small table with a drawer, you can easily create your own piece of magic furniture using a tablecloth, a stool and a couple of bulldog clips.

**1** Place the tablecloth over the table or stool, making sure that most of the fabric falls to one side. You now need to bunch and gather this fabric in order to make a loose pouch out of it.

Props:
Small bulldog clips
Small table or stool
Large tablecloth

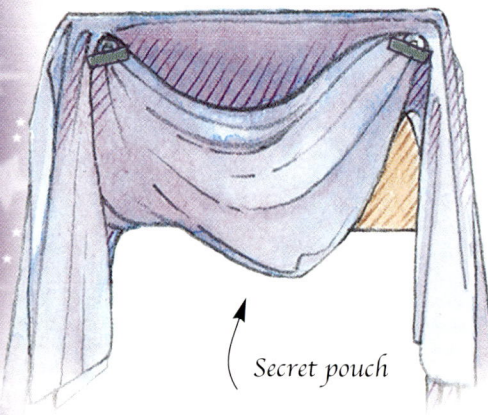

Secret pouch

**2** Hold the pouch in place with the bulldog clips, making sure that neither the clips nor the pouch are visible to your audience. This will allow you to drop or pick things up from your secret place.

# Time for Tricks

# Cauldron Code

## Reveal the colour of a hidden cauldron!

**1** First, you have to remember the cauldron code: the colours red, orange and yellow are each worth one and colours blue, green and black are each worth nil. Trace over the cauldron-shaped templates on page 60 of this book and cut them out. Colour them as stated.

*Props:*
White card
Felt-tip pens
(red, orange, yellow, green, blue, black)
Scissors
Handkerchief

**2** Place the cauldrons on the table and secretly add up the values of the colours showing. For example, if the colours showing are red, green and yellow, remember the number two (red = 1, green = 0, yellow = 1).

## Wizard's Tip

*Remember which colours are paired on each cauldron.*

**3** Ask a volunteer to turn any number of cauldrons over, one at a time, while your back is turned. Each time the spectator turns one of the cauldrons they must say "turn".

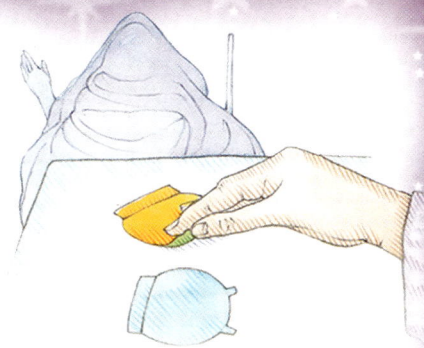

**4** Each time the spectator says "turn", add one to the number you started with. So, if the person made six turns and you had started with 2, you would end up with the number 8. When the spectator has finished, ask them to hide one cauldron with the handkerchief.

**5** If the number you ended up with is an even number, then the values of the colours facing up will also be even. This works the same for odd numbers.

**6** From the two colours that are not covered you can work out the colour that is hidden. For example, if your final number is odd, and blue and yellow are visible (which is also odd: blue = 0, yellow = 1) the hidden colour has to be green.

### Wizard's Tip
It sounds a bit complicated, but practising a few times with your eyes shut will soon help you to get the hang of it.

# Vanishing Pouch

Meldrick's magic cloak produced many amazing objects, but the vanishing pouch was the most magnificent. Bythia the Wanderer asked for a small piece of the cloak to make the amazing pouch.

1. From a distance, show the audience the inside of your vanishing pouch. Be sure to hold open the secret area. The audience sees the pouch as dark and empty.

Props:
Wizard's Pouch from kit
Coin

2. Invite an audience member to examine the coin. Now, ask them to drop the coin in the bag. Be sure to hold open the secret compartment.

**3** Wave your hands over the pouch and say your magic words. Bythia said, "Dibbity, dabbity, dobbity, go!" While you are doing this, flip the secret compartment closed, which will hide the coin.

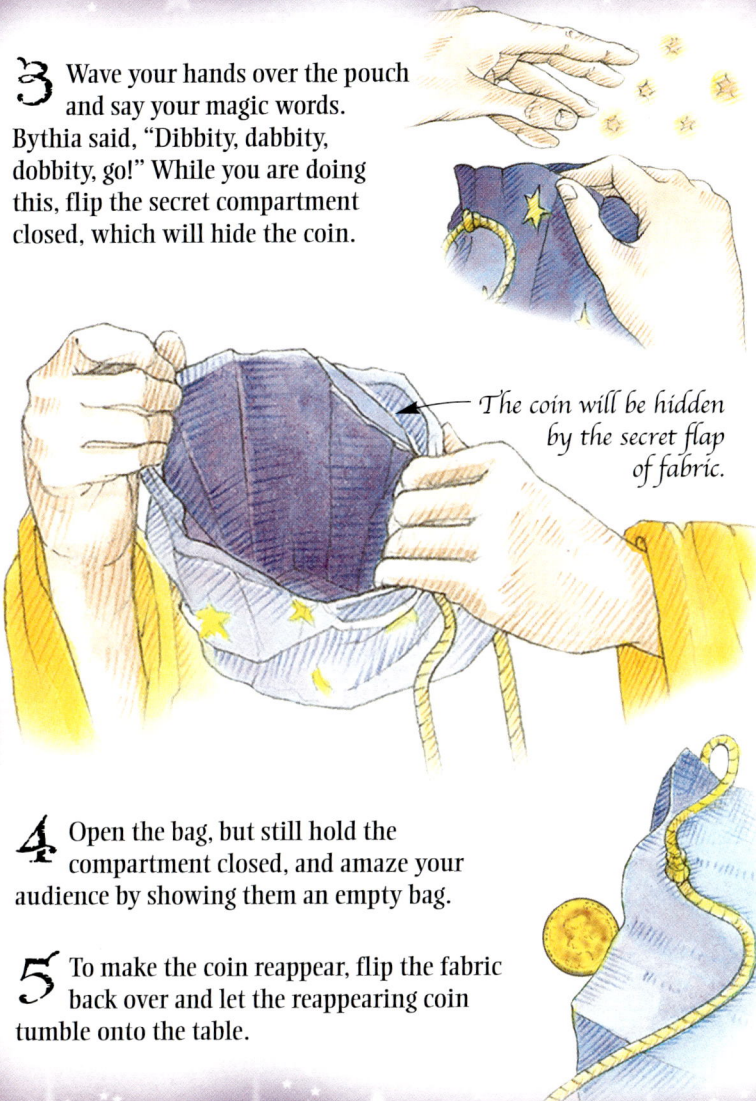

*The coin will be hidden by the secret flap of fabric.*

**4** Open the bag, but still hold the compartment closed, and amaze your audience by showing them an empty bag.

**5** To make the coin reappear, flip the fabric back over and let the reappearing coin tumble onto the table.

# Crystal Ball

Make a magical crystal ball move across a table top, following your every command!

**1** Your apprentice needs to be in on the trick too, so brief them before you begin. Tie the 2m length of cotton onto the ring.

*Props:*
*Apprentice*
*Table*
*Tablecloth*
*Plain ring*
*2m length of thread*
*Glass marble*

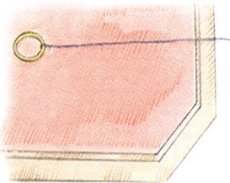

**2** Place the ring onto the table with the thread trailing across to the opposite side. Cover the table and the ring with the tablecloth, ensuring that your assistant holds the thread.

**3** Tell your audience that you will make a magical crystal ball move under your command. As you say this, hold up the marble for everyone to see.

**4** Place the crystal ball (marble) into the hidden ring and say a wizard's spell, such as: 'Magical, mystical crystal ball, under my spell you must fall!' Your assistant should then carefully pull the thread which is attached to the ring.

**5** As the marble is pulled across the table, look as if you are really concentrating. When it is nearly at the edge, your assistant must stop pulling so you can pick up the marble for your audience to examine – amazing!

### Wizard's Tip
Whilst your audience is examining the marble, your assistant should dispose of the evidence by placing it in their pocket.

# Magic Mirror

Discovered by the Raven in the ice caverns of Alcatron, this trick was brought to Meldrick and is known to the wizarding world as the "Magic Mirror".

**Props:**
Mirror
Soap
Paper
Pen

**1** Before you perform this trick, write the number 18 on your mirror using soap.

**2** Ask for a volunteer from your audience and have them write down any three digit number. Each digit must be a different number.

**3** Next, ask the volunteer to reverse their chosen numbers and write it down underneath the first. Ask them to subtract the smaller number from the larger, and write it down.

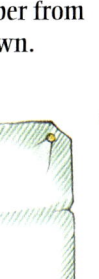

**4** Get them to reverse the answer and add it to their last number and write it down. Ask the volunteer to add all the digits together from the final answer.

**5** Say your magic wizard's spell. The Raven said to Meldrick, "Mirror, mirror on the wall, reveal the number to them all!" Breathe on the mirror to have your magical answer appear. To the audience's amazement, the answer will show up. What the audience doesn't know is that the answer will always be 18.

# Morphology

## Change a mere copper coin into a silver one!

**Props:**
One copper coin
One silver coin
Paper

1. Copy the template for the magic wallet on page 62.

2. Glue the centre pieces together. When dried, open out one of the sheets, place a silver coin in the centre and fold the paper, following the lines on the template, so that it covers the coin.

3. Turn the wallet over and open out the other sheet – you are now ready to perform the trick.

4. Show the audience the sheet of paper and place the copper coin in its centre. Fold the paper over the coin as in step 2.

5. On the very last fold turn the whole packet over. Wave your hand over the packet and then open it out to reveal the silver coin – alacazam!

# Metamorphosis

Create the illusion that a solid object is flexible.

**Props:** Wooden pencil

1. Bang the pencil on the wall or on a table to prove that it is solid.

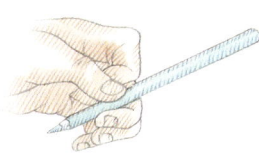

2. Ask a member of your audience to inspect the pencil to prove that it is solid.

3. Loosely hold the pencil against your thumb and middle finger at the pointed end.

4. Rapidly shake your hand up and down. Make sure that you only move it a little bit in either direction and the pencil will look as if it is made of rubber.

## Wizard's Tip

Whenever you perform a simple trick like Metamorphosis, quickly move onto the next trick so that the audience doesn't have time to work it out.

# Octagon Oracle

## Read someone's mind with the help of the octagon oracles!

**1** Using the template on page 61, draw five equal-sized octagon shapes onto the card and cut them out. In your best wizard's writing, write the numbers onto each of the octagons, as shown.

*Props:*
*Card*
*Black pen*
*Scissors*

Yellow octagon:
12  8
7  1  11
13  6

Blue octagon:
14  12
8  4  13
9  7

Green octagon:
14  11
10  5  12
6  13

Red octagon:
7  14
12  2  11
10  9

Yellow octagon:
8  14
10  3  9
13  11

**2** Hand the octagons to a member of the audience and ask them to think of a number from one to fourteen. They must keep the number a secret.

**3** Tell the volunteer to hand back to you all of the octagons which bear the number being thought.

**4.** Say a wizard's spell such as: "Octagon Oracles lend me your might, and help me to gain profound insight."
Whilst you are doing this, secretly add together the centre numbers on all of the octagons you have been given. Your total will be the chosen number!

**5.** Announce the chosen number to the amazement of your volunteer!

## Wizard's Tip
Make your cards look really ancient by dipping them in cold tea when the ink is dry.

# Wizard Stars

Pendragon the Peacemaker descended from the clouds at the Wizard's Council to reveal how to transform an egg into wizard's stars!

Props:
Egg
Toothpick
Stars from kit
Glue
Cloth

1. Make a small hole at each end of the egg using the toothpick. Very gently blow out the contents of the egg into a bowl. Ask an adult for help, if you need it.

2. Once the inside of the egg is clean, carefully fill it with the stars. Seal the holes with a small dab of glue. Smooth out the glue so you can't see it.

*Roll up a paper funnel to help you fill the egg with the stars.*

3. Place the egg on the table, and cover it with the cloth.

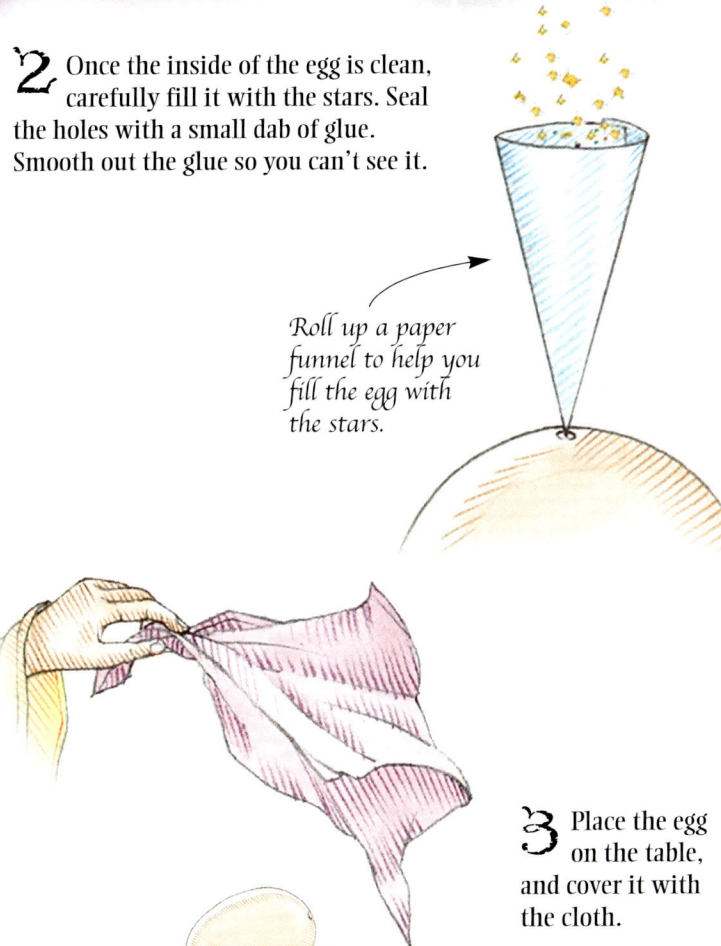

**4.** Say a wizard's spell like the one Pendragon said, "Bright lights beyond the Moon and Mars, change the contents of this egg from yolk to stars!"

**5.** As you say this, bash your hand down on top of the covered egg, smashing it to pieces.

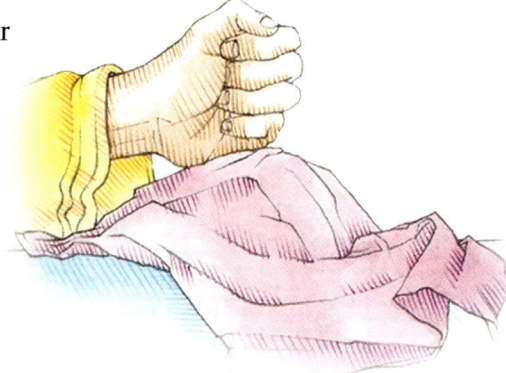

**6** Shake the cloth in the air, so the stars fly at your audience.

### Wizard's Tip
This trick works even better if you can hide the egg in someone's fridge first. Then, perform it in front of them!

# Coin Elevation

Use your powers of wizardry to balance a coin on your fingertips. No-one else in the room will be able to do this.

1. Secretly place the pin lengthways between the first two fingers of your dominant hand.

**Props:**
Coin
Straight pin

2. Now hand the coin around your audience, allowing them to inspect it. You could even borrow a coin for the trick.

3. Maintaining pressure on the pin, raise the coin to balance it in a standing position. The coin will balance as if held by magical forces!

4. Invite people from the audience to try and balance the coin – they will not be able to do it.

# Evanescence

Make a small object or coin disappear in front of an astounded audience!

Props:
Coin or small object
Table
Sleeve

**1** Tell your audience that you are able to make an object vanish by rubbing it against your elbow. Now attempt to show this, but allow it to fall off the table.

**2** Tell your audience that it usually works better with the other elbow. Now, being very discreet, pretend to place the object into your other hand. As you raise your elbow, allow it to slide down your opposite sleeve.

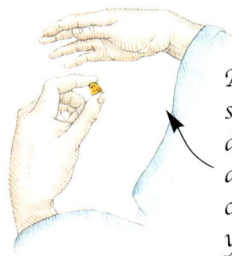

As you swap hands, discreetly drop the object down your sleeve.

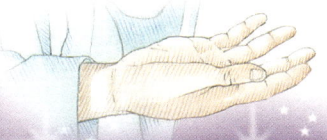

**3** As you rub your elbow and palm together, show the audience that the object has disappeared!

# Potion Prediction

## From a possible six, correctly predict a volunteer's chosen concoction!

The secret behind the trick is the fact that each of the potions contains a different number of letters. The template for your cards can be found on page 63 of this book.

**1.** Spread the cards out face-up on the table, and ask your volunteer to select one and memorise it. They must now turn all the cards over, and shuffle them.

Props:
Brown card labelled Elixir
Purple card labelled Fire Water
Green card labelled Lava
Blue card labelled Spirita
Red card labelled Truth
Yellow card labelled Dew

**2.** Spread the cards out on the table again, but this time, face-down. Ask your volunteer to spell out silently one letter of their chosen potion each time you tap a card. When he reaches the last letter of his potion, he must yell "stop!" For the first two letters of the potion, you can tap any card on the table, but on the third tap you must select the potion with three letters, on the fourth, the potion with four letters, and so on.

Fire Water  Lava  Elixir  Spirita  Dew  Truth

*Remember which colour card corresponds to each spell.*

**3.** It will work out that when your volunteer yells "stop!", you will be tapping the card featuring the name of his potion – as all the others have been eliminated! Yet because the cards on the table are not positioned in sequence, this will not be obvious to your audience.

# Wizard's Squeeze

Defy mortal logic by making two pints squeeze into one.

**1.** Place the two pint glasses, jug of water and the bag of sawdust onto the table and tell your audience that you will make two pints squeeze into one.

Props:
Two pint glasses
Jug of water
Table
Bag of sawdust

2. Carefully fill one glass with water and the other with sawdust. It will improve your performance if you can tell your audience a wizard's tale or joke whilst you are doing this.

3. Utter a wizard's spell such as, "Defying logic is a breeze, if you perform the wizard's squeeze!" Whilst you are doing this, pour the glass of water into the pint of sawdust.

### Wizard's Tip
To make the magic seem more dramatic, turn the glass which held the water upside down once you have finished the trick.

4. Your audience will be amazed to see that two pints squeeze into one!

# Ropology

## Make a knot magically appear at the end of a piece of rope!

**1** Secretly tie a knot at the end of a piece of rope or string. If your rope has knots at both ends, untie one of them.

*Don't let anyone see the knot.*

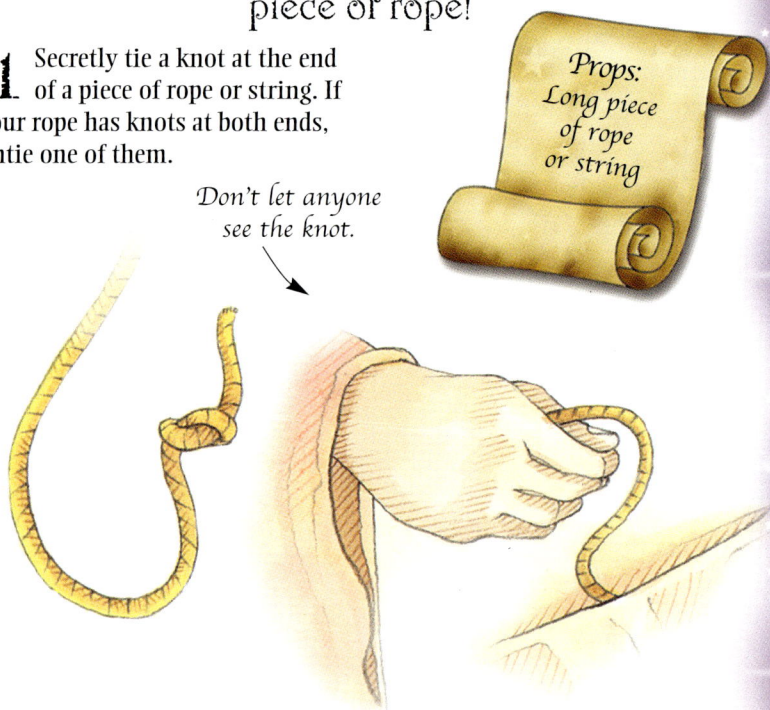

**Props:** Long piece of rope or string

**2** When your wizard friends have arrived to see your magic performance, pull the prepared rope out of your pocket. Make sure that you conceal the knot in your hand as shown.

**3** Tell your audience that you are going to use your wizardly powers to make a knot appear in the piece of rope. Whilst you are talking, grasp the other end of the rope with your free hand.

**4** After a lengthy pause release the unknotted end of the rope.

**5** Gather up the end again, tell your audience that you need complete silence in order for this trick to work.

**6** Release the end of the rope again, but this time release the end with the knot. Take a bow.

### Wizard's Tip
Simple tricks often work best. Do not repeat tricks as it will make it easier for your audience to work out what you are doing.

# Wizard's Brew

Nedroc was a wizard in love with the magic of food. He made a special brew for the entire Wizard's Council. Here's how he turned ordinary water into a colourful concoction.

**Props:**
Dark coloured mug
Green food colouring
Jug filled with water
Glass

**1** Before your performance, put three or four drops of green food colouring in the dark coloured mug. Shake it around so that it covers the base and the sides. Then, allow it to dry.

**2** Show your audience the insides of the mug. Once the food colouring is dry, it will be invisible.

**3** Place the mug on the floor and pour the water into it. Pour it while you are standing up, this will help mix the water and food colouring. As you are pouring, say the wizard spell, like Nedroc, "Wizards are always kind not mean, so turn this water from clear to green."

*The water will turn green.*

**4** Now, pour the water in the mug into the empty glass. To your audience's amazement the water will be green.

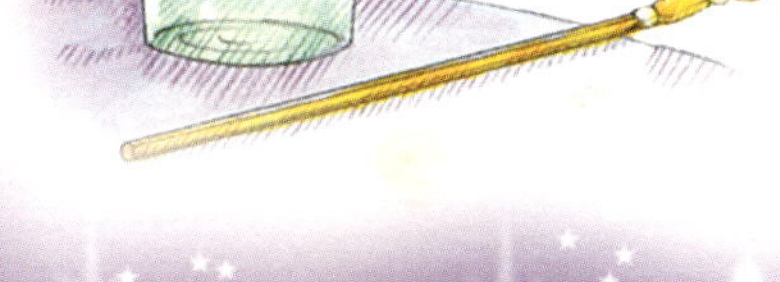

### Raven's Tip
You can use other colours of food colouring too. Try red or blue. Or you can have two dark mugs and mix different colours together. Experiment and have fun!

# Enchanted Key

## Call on the help of your wizard forefathers to make a key turn over in your hand.

*Props: Large Key*

**1** Place the key across the palm of your hand. The part of the key which goes in the keyhole should be pointing towards you. The end which you turn must not touch your hand at all.

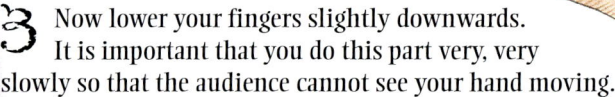

**2** Tell your audience to be very quiet, as you have to summon the help of your wizard forefathers.

**3** Now lower your fingers slightly downwards. It is important that you do this part very, very slowly so that the audience cannot see your hand moving.

**4** To the astonishment of your audience the key will now roll over. Your wizard forefathers have helped you out once again!

*Slowly lower your fingers.*

### Wizard's Tip
Make the key move as slowly as possible, as this will give the appearance that an unseen entity is intervening and helping with the trick.

# Mind Meeting

An audience member selects a random object from the room. When you return, your amazing powers of wizardry ensure you can name this mystery object.

**1** Before you perform the trick, arrange a set of signals between yourself and an accomplice. For instance, if your audience member selects a blue object, your accomplice will scratch their nose; if the object is yellow, they will touch their hair. Now leave the room.

*Props: An accomplice*

**2** Your accomplice will escort an audience member around the room, acting as your assistant. When the object has been chosen, you will re-enter the room – and remembering the secret signals, will be able to name the chosen object.

*Wizard's Tip*
This is a trick you can play on more than one audience member, so have fun!

# Ancient Runes

These runes were sealed inside a Pharaoh's tomb for thousands of years. Mustapha the Mystic astounded all his fellow wizards with the magical powers of his rune stones.

Props:
Runes from the kit
Paper
Pen

**1** Copy the ten magical runes from the template on page 64.

**2** Choose one of the rune stones and write down the symbols on a piece of paper. Fold the paper and put it on your table. Put the rest of the stones on the table too, except for the chosen stone. Put the chosen stone in your pocket. You are ready to do the trick.

**3** Show the stones to your audience and mix them up on the table.

**4** Now, ask someone to lay the stones out in a row so the like symbols touch. All the stones must be used.

**5** Ask everyone to look at the symbols at each end of the row. Now, open the paper that has been sitting on the table and show it to your audience. They'll be amazed that the symbols are the same.

### Wizard's Tip

If you take one card from the set and the others are laid out with like pictures touching, the designs at the ends of the row will always match those of the card that has been taken out!

# Magic Magnetism

Make a dessert spoon appear to hover in the air. This is an ideal trick to perform at the dinner table!

**1** Interweave your fingers, as shown in the picture below.

*Props: One dessert spoon*

**2** Arrange your fingers so that the middle finger of one hand is looser than the rest.

**3** Now pick up the dessert spoon, placing it behind the loose finger as shown. Use your thumbs to hold the top of the spoon – they will look like they are holding it in place.

**4** Say a magic spell such as: "Wizam, wizo, wizard!" and with a look of great concentration, remove your thumbs from the end of the spoon. It will look as if the spoon is being held in the air by a magical force!

**5** After a few moments, drop the spoon and allow the audience to examine your hands and the spoon.

# Rings of Moebius

Magically link, multiply and enlarge rings using only a pair of scissors.

1. Cut three strips of paper, each measuring 25 cm by 2.5 cm.

*Props:*
*Scissors*
*Paper*
*Glue*

2. Stick the ends of the first strip together to make a loop. Secure with glue.

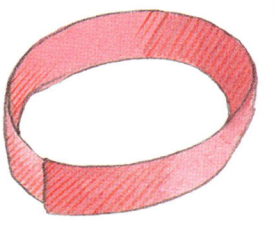

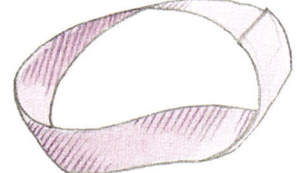

3. Twist the second strip once before gluing the ends together.

4. Take the third strip and twist it twice before gluing the ends together.

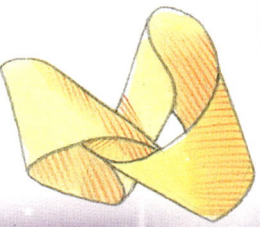

**5** Say a wizard's spell such as: "Rings of Moebius, your time has come, after each cut the transformation will be done." Pierce each strip in the centre and cut along the loop lengthways.

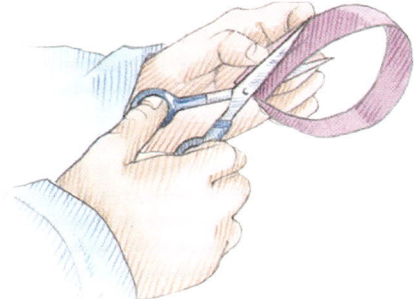

**6** The first strip will become two separate loops. The second loop becomes twice its original size. The third loop becomes two loops linked together!

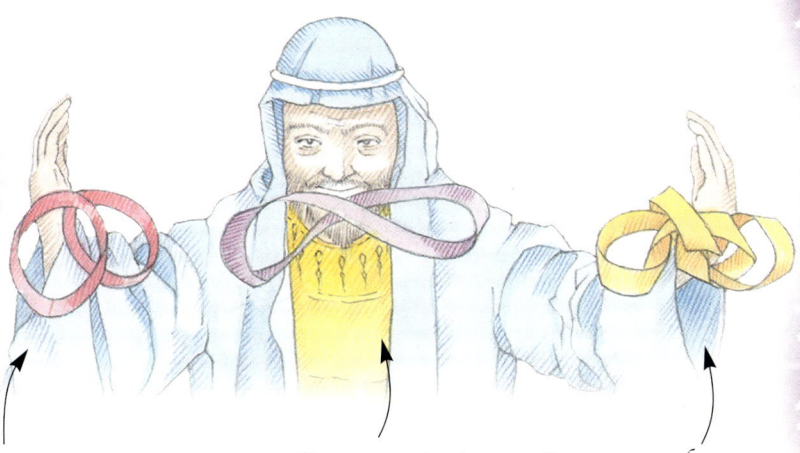

*Becomes two separate loops of paper.*

*Becomes twice its original length.*

*Becomes two loops linked together.*

# Midas Touch

Many moons ago, elder wizards spoke of a man who had the ability to transform everything he touched into gold. Master the modern equivalent by transforming one bank note into six!

Props:
Six bank notes

**1.** Before the performance, roll up five bank notes into a very tight bundle.

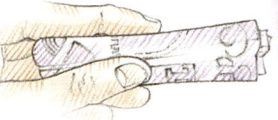

**2.** Secretly place the rolled notes into the crease of your left elbow. Use the folds in your sleeve to conceal the notes and keep your arm bent.

Conceal the bank notes.

### Wizard's Tip
Wear a long-flowing robe or dressing gown to help you conceal the rolled bank notes.

**3** It is now time to perform the trick. Hold the remaining note with your right hand so that the audience can see it clearly.

**4** While you are showing the audience that there is nothing hidden in the note, roll up the sleeve of your left arm with your right hand and transfer the note into your left hand. At the same time, with your right hand, secretly collect the concealed notes from your elbow.

**5** Bring both of your hands together and place the five rolled notes behind the single note.

**6** Unroll the notes and count them off one by one. Your audience will think that you have the Midas touch!

# Wizard's Range

Amaze your audience by being the only wizard able to spin an egg properly! Others will try, but fail.

**1.** Ask an adult to prepare a hardboiled egg for you.

*Props: Five eggs, one of which is hardboiled. Bowl*

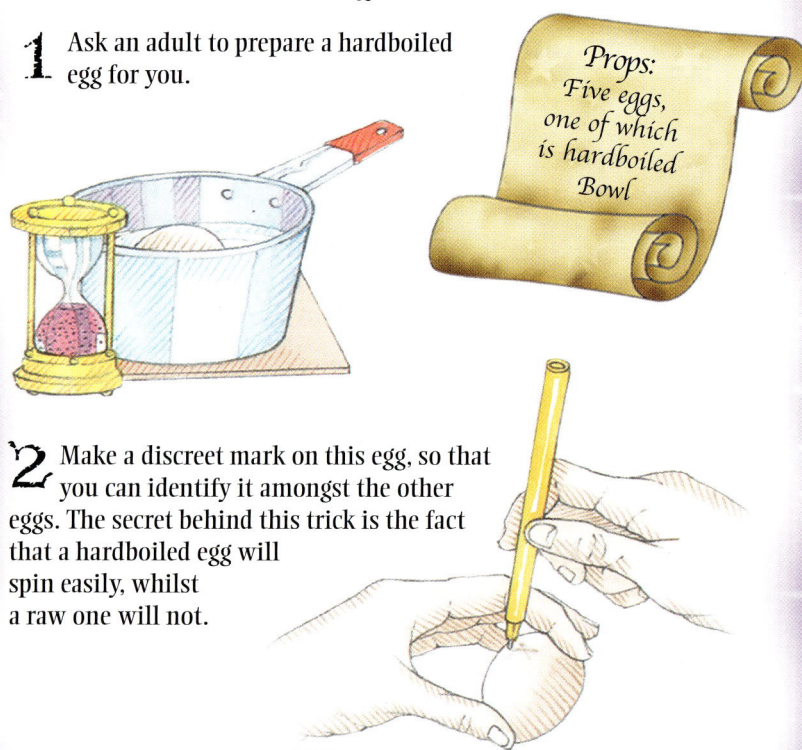

**2.** Make a discreet mark on this egg, so that you can identify it amongst the other eggs. The secret behind this trick is the fact that a hardboiled egg will spin easily, whilst a raw one will not.

**3** Ask a volunteer to choose an egg from the bowl of five you have prepared. If he or she chooses the hardboiled one, say that will be yours to spin and ask them to choose another. If your volunteer chooses a raw one, then select the hardboiled one for yourself.

*Only the hardboiled egg will spin.*

**4** Now spin! Your egg should rotate easily and evenly. Ask your volunteer to do the same. They won't be able to, however hard they try!

# Magic Maths

Using your mystical powers of duplication, double the amount of coins placed on a magazine before the eyes of your audience.

Props:
Six identical coins
Magazine

**1** The secret behind this trick is preparation! Before you perform, place three of the coins under the cover of the magazine. Put the magazine on the table until you are ready to perform the trick.

**2** Now place the remaining three coins on the cover of the magazine.

**3** Carefully pick up the magazine with one hand, whilst showing your other hand to the audience to prove that it is empty. The hidden coins and the coins on the cover should fall into the hand holding the magazine.

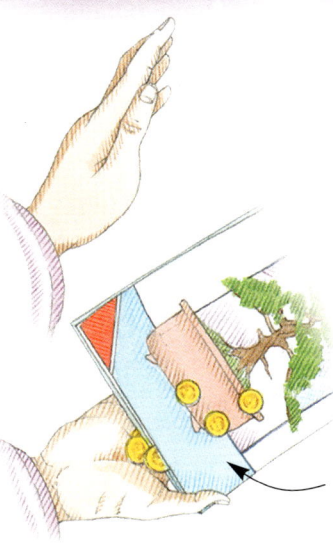

*Discreetly let the hidden coins fall into your hand.*

**4** Say a wizard's spell such as: "By the wizardly powers entrusted to me, change three coins to six for all to see!" When you open your palm, you can reveal six coins instead of the expected three!

# Vanishing Point

Learn how to vanish like a ghost with this simple but effective piece of wizardry.

**1** You stand in the doorway facing your audience, who are in the room. Inform them that you are about to make yourself disappear!

**Props:** Sheet or blanket (large enough to cover an open doorway)

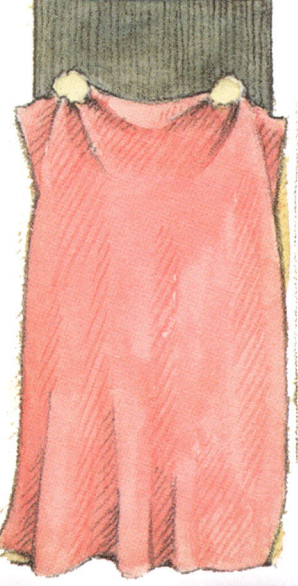

**2** Slowly lift the blanket up in front of you until it is over your head.

**3** Hold your hands out wide so the blanket also covers the whole of the doorway.

**4** Keeping your hands still, move as much of your body sideways as you possibly can. Say a wizard's spell such as: "Ladies and gentlemen, do not fear, I am about to make myself disappear!"

**5** The next bit is tricky as you have to drop the blanket and move your arms and body out of the doorframe at the same time. If you achieve this it will look as though you have disappeared. Although this trick is very simple, it requires a lot of practice to get it right.

### Wizard's Tip
You may have to run fast, but it is a good idea to come back into the room through a different doorway if you can. This makes the trick even more baffling.

# Potion Trickery

Perform this prank to charm any soothsayer.

**Props:**
Plastic cup filled with water
Blindfold
Straw

1. Before the performance, place a long drinking straw in your pocket.

2. Select a volunteer from the audience and tell them that you will make a cup filled with water disappear whilst they are holding it. Place the blindfold over your volunteer's eyes and ask them to hold the cup on their head.

3. To the amusement of your audience, retrieve the drinking straw from your pocket and proceed to quietly drink the water. Be careful not to touch the volunteer's hands or head, as this will alert them to what's happening.

4. After you have finished the water, take off the volunteer's blindfold and take a bow.

## Wizard's Tip
Use humour in your wizard routines; making your audience laugh can be used to distract them when you are performing.

# Templates and Tokens

On the following pages, you'll find the templates which you need to use in the tricks included in this book. Simply trace around them onto card or thick paper, and cut out and colour them as they appear here.

# Cauldron Code

These cauldron templates are for use in the Cauldron Code trick on page 16.

Colour the reverse side blue.   Colour the reverse side green.

Colour the reverse side black.

# Octagon Oracle

These octagons are intended for use with the Octagon Oracle trick on page 26.

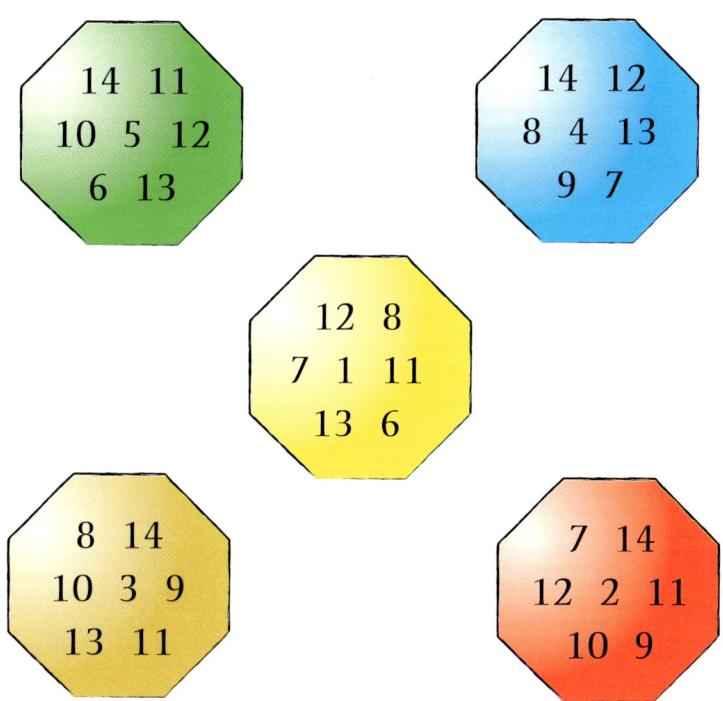

# Morphology

This is the template for the magic wallet, required for the Morphology trick on page 24. You will need to make two copies in order to perform the trick.

# Potion Prediction

Copy these potion cards and use them for the Potion Prediction trick on page 34.

| | |
|---|---|
| Elixir | Fire Water |
| Spirita | Dew |
| Lava | Truth |

# Ancient Runes

Trace and then cut out these ancient runes for use with the trick on page 44.

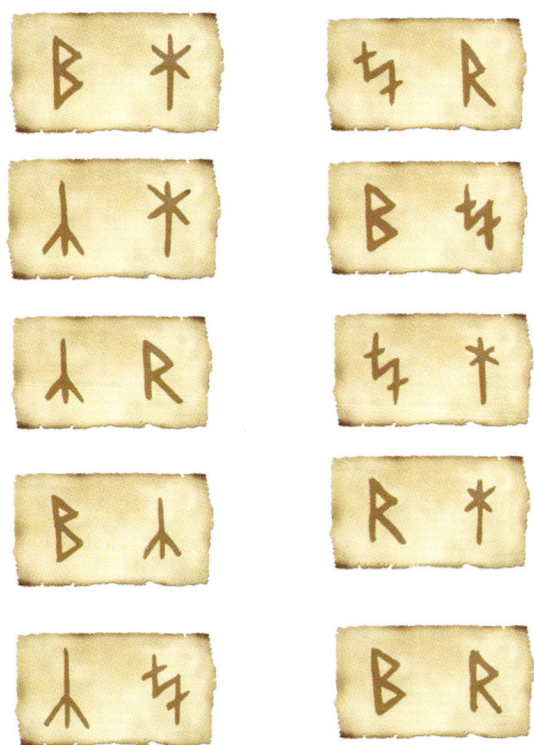